Myths, Magic and Legends

A Step-by-Step Guide for the Aspiring Myth-Maker

Tony Tallarico

Dover Publications, Inc.
Mineola, New York

Bibliographical Note

This Dover edition, first published in 2009, is an unabridged republication of the work originally published by The Berkley Publishing Group, New York, in 1994.

Library of Congress Cataloging-in-Publication Data

Tallarico, Tony, 1933–
    Drawing and cartooning myths, magic, and legends : a step-by-step guide for the aspiring myth-maker / Tony Tallarico. — Dover ed.
        p. cm.
    Originally published: New York : Berkley Pub. Group, 1994.
    ISBN-13: 978-0-486-47277-5 (pbk.)
    ISBN-10: 0-486-47277-9 (pbk.)
    1. Art and mythology—Juvenile literature. 2. Drawing—Technique—Juvenile literature. 3. Cartooning—Technique—Juvenile literature. I. Title.

NC825.M9T36 2009
741.2—dc22

                                                        2009026193

Manufactured in the United States by Courier Corporation
47277901
www.doverpublications.com

You are all welcome to enter a time of myths, magic and legends. Prepare for battle (and a few laughs too) by sharpening your pencil, making sure your marker is not dry and by carrying a sufficient supply of paper.

— Onward —

tony tallarico

This book on drawing and cartooning myths, magic and legends must begin with the all-time star of magic . . .

MERLIN

No matter how involved this drawing appears, by following the simple steps on the facing page you can create your own picture of Merlin.

1— Draw the basic shape lightly in pencil.

2— Add additional shapes lightly in pencil.

3— Continue adding basic shapes lightly in pencil.

4— Using a felt-tip pen, complete the drawing. Erase all the pencil lines.

Once you've completed the four basic steps above, you can add more details and black areas to your finished drawing. Never add these details until you are ready.

EVIL MONSTER

This is a simple line drawing. No blacks or shadows have been used.

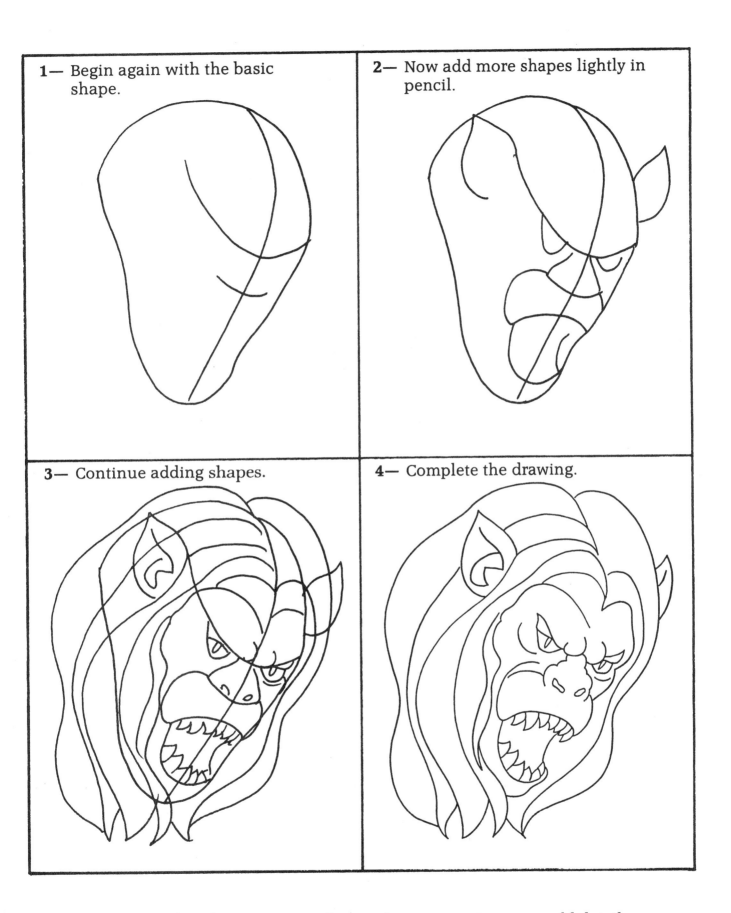

1— Begin again with the basic shape.

2— Now add more shapes lightly in pencil.

3— Continue adding shapes.

4— Complete the drawing.

Follow the four basic steps as shown above . . . again, never add details until you are happy with your basic shapes.

SORCERESS

Again, this is a simple line drawing without the use of blacks or shadows.

8

STEP 1—

STEP 2—

STEP 3—

STEP 4—

Carefully place the basic shapes in their correct positions and don't be afraid to erase or draw through the shapes.
Now let's add some blacks and shadows . . .

9

LIGHT AND SHADOWS

You can make any drawing more dynamic and interesting by establishing a light source and then putting in shadows from that light source.
You can use either a brush and black India ink or a black marker to draw the shadows.
Wherever light strikes the form, leave white. Be aware of cast shadows.
You can also soften a shadow by feathering it into the light source.
Notice how each drawing changes its appearance as a result of different light sources.

Light source

Light source

Light
source

Light
source

Light
source

You can also use blacks in a decorative manner without a light source.

MYTHICAL CREATURE

Light source

Cast shadow

When you wish to soften your shadows always feather toward the light source.

Try drawing this same flying dragon with a different light source.

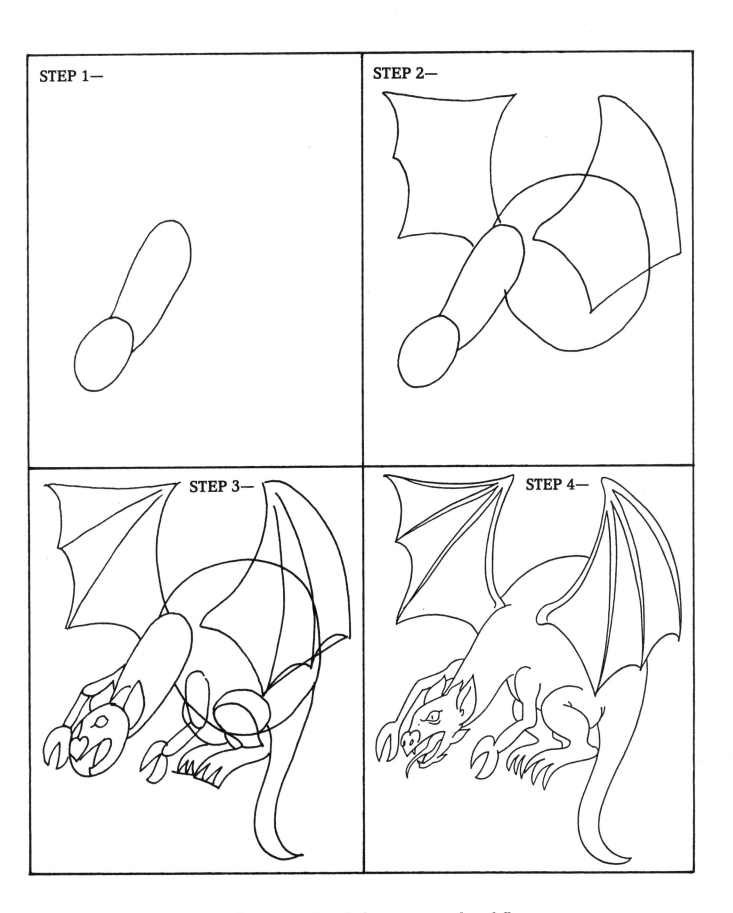

STEP 1—

STEP 2—

STEP 3—

STEP 4—

Whether you're drawing a head, figure or mythical flying creature, the steps are always the same.

NESTOR WITH THE MAGIC SWORD

The light source is the glow from the sword.

By placing the greatest amount of shadows and blacks, the sword becomes spotlighted.

In step 3, draw the arm and hand shapes first before
drawing the sword shape.

WILD BEAST

Light
source

The lighting in this figure has been
kept simple by using a heavy line
on the shadow side only.

16

STEP 1—

STEP 2—

STEP 3—

STEP 4—

Keep drawing these simple shapes and don't be afraid to erase—
the Wild Beast will never know.

17

THE KEEPER OF
THE DUNGEON

Shadows do not always have to be put in with big, heavy black areas. Interesting drawings can be made using line patterns only. In this drawing only parallel lines were used.

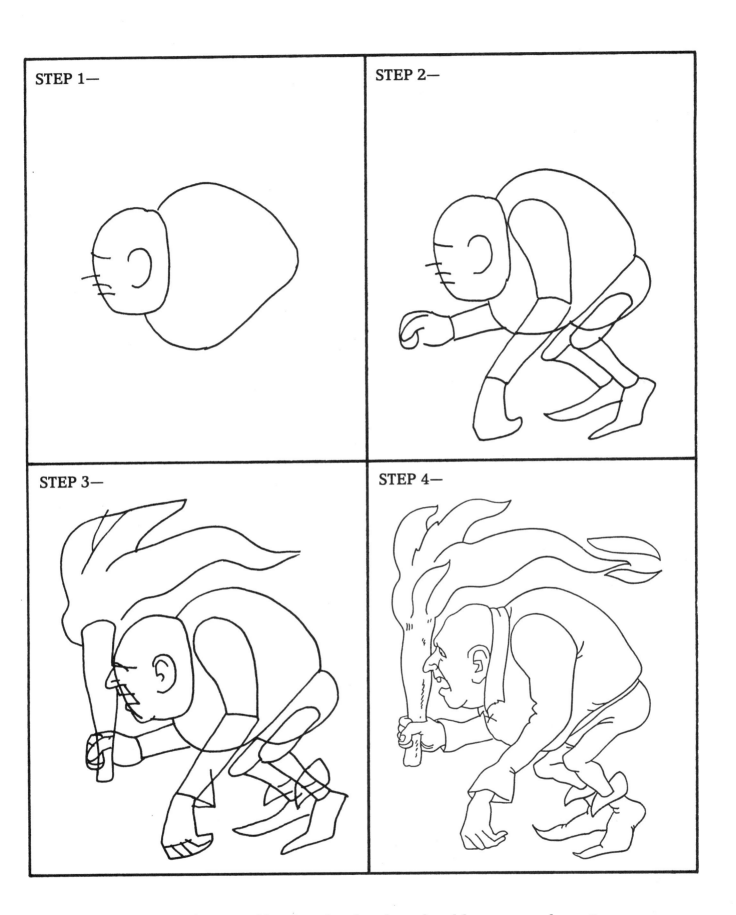

STEP 1—

STEP 2—

STEP 3—

STEP 4—

From the top of his head to his feet should measure about 2 head shapes high.

THE HOODED KNIGHT

Light shadow

Medium shadow

Dark shadow

Darkest shadow

The shadows in this drawing were put in with 4 line patterns only— no solid blacks.

STEP 1—

STEP 2—

STEP 3—

STEP 4—

As shown in step 2, this figure measures approximately 8 head shapes high.

21

THE LEADER OF THE WING-CLAN

Short, slightly curved strokes give the impression of fur or hair.

This drawing was completed using line patterns and blacks.

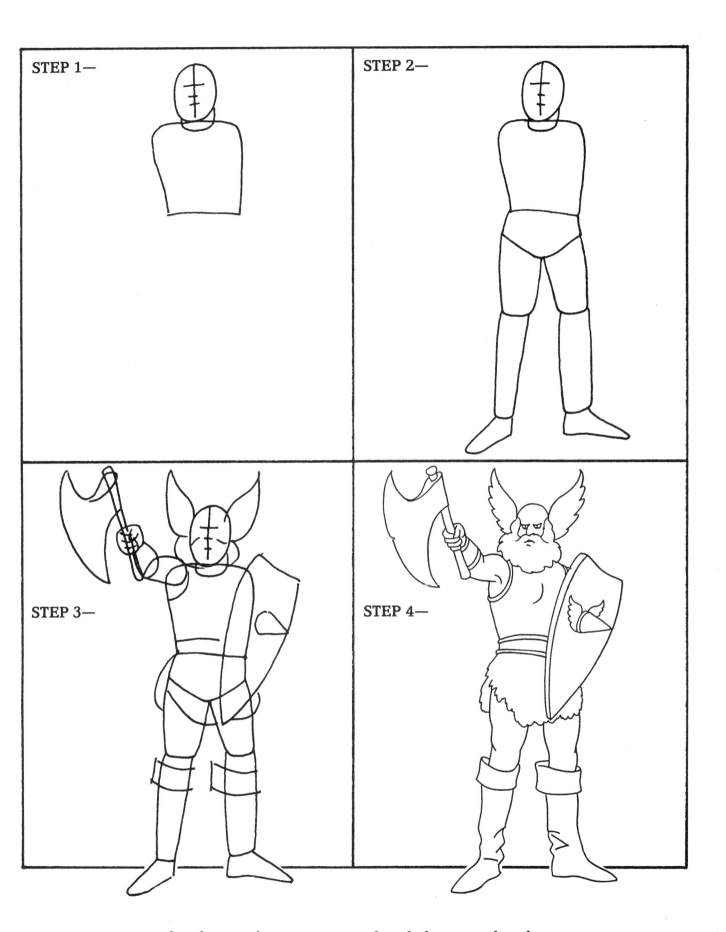

STEP 1—

STEP 2—

STEP 3—

STEP 4—

This figure also measures 8 head shapes in height.

ZEUS

This drawing was completed
using solid blacks in a
design pattern rather
than working from a
source of light.

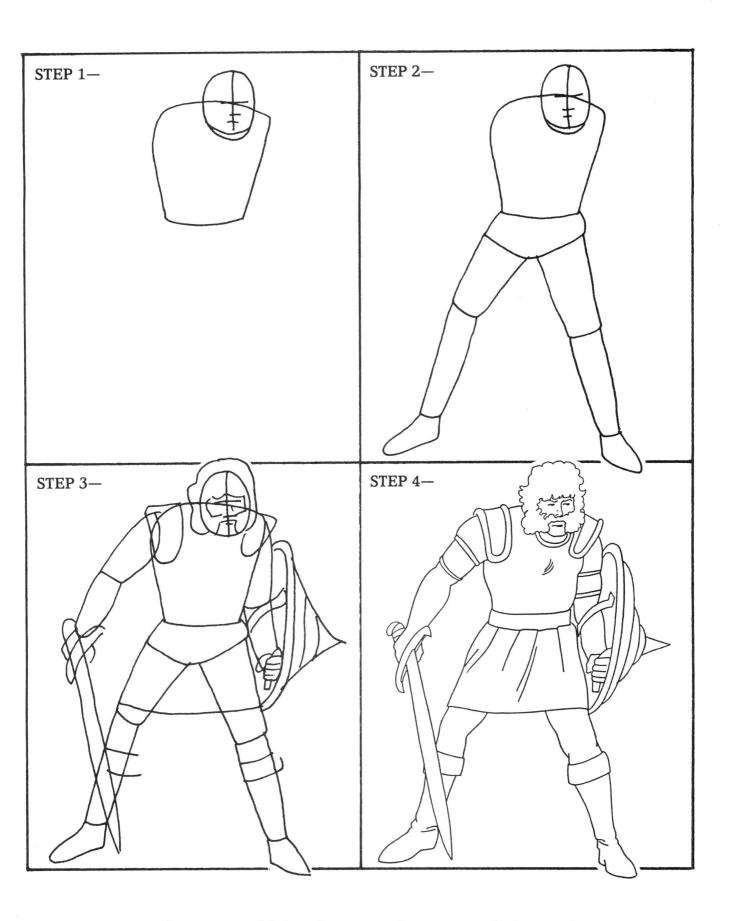

STEP 1—

STEP 2—

STEP 3—

STEP 4—

Remember not to add details in your drawing until after you have
completed all the basic shapes lightly in pencil.

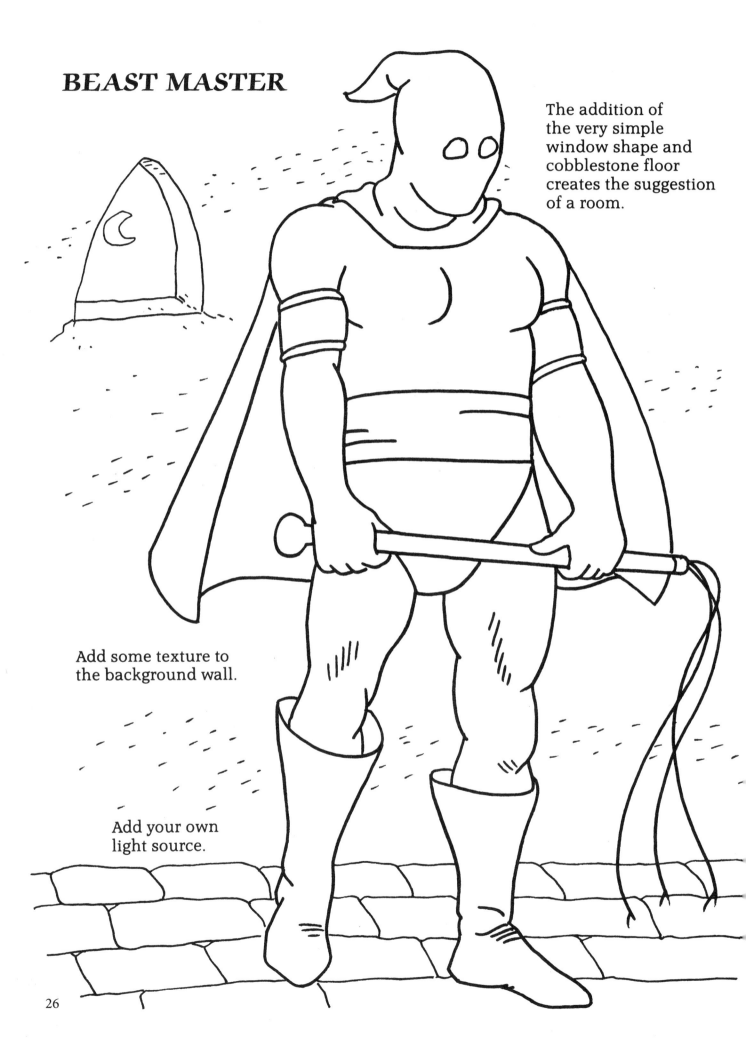

BEAST MASTER

The addition of the very simple window shape and cobblestone floor creates the suggestion of a room.

Add some texture to the background wall.

Add your own light source.

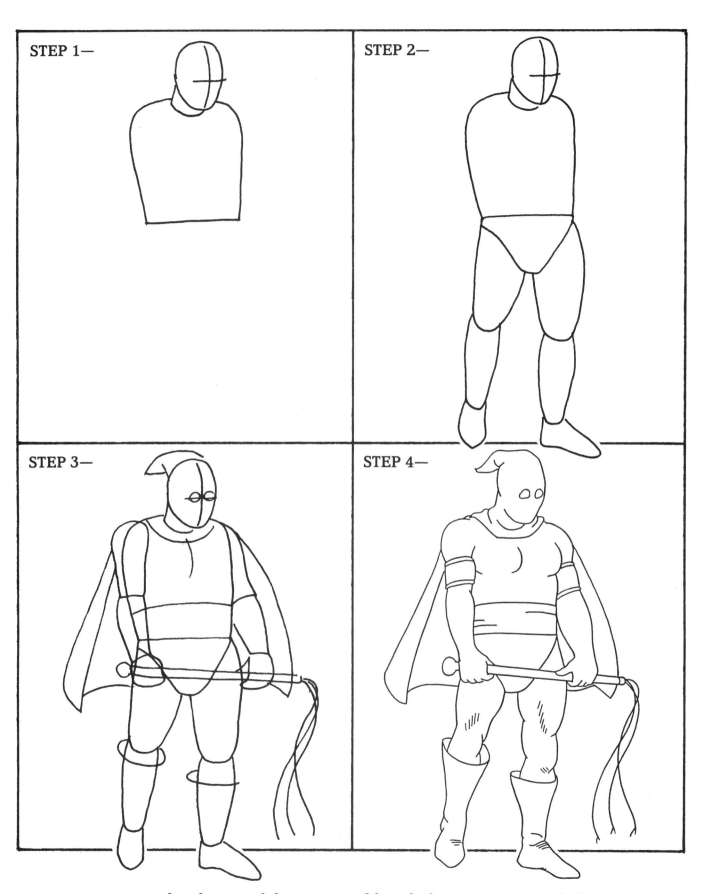

STEP 1—

STEP 2—

STEP 3—

STEP 4—

Draw in the shapes of the arms and hands first, as in step 3, before placing the whip shape in position.

READY FOR
BATTLE

Front-side light source

Add a few boulders and some weeds to establish a ground area.

STEP 1—

STEP 2—

STEP 3—

STEP 4—

This figure measures about 6 head shapes high. The average male figure is about 6½ head shapes high.

A FOREST WARRIOR

Strong
light
source

Some liberties must be
taken with the shadows
to preserve the form—
see the right arm area.

STEP 1—

STEP 2—

STEP 3—

STEP 4—

Always draw the figure shapes before placing whatever items they are holding.

31

CHARGE

A simple curve
establishes a
ground line.

A burst of energy is formed
by drawing all the background
lines to one point—see dot
on belt.

32

STEP 1—

STEP 2—

STEP 3—

STEP 4—

Don't be afraid to draw through shapes—a good example of this is his cape in step 3.

ANCIENT DRAGON SLAYER

This is an example of a figure drawn in line only with a very slight suggestion of shadows.

Add rough ground lines with some texture.

34

STEP 1—

STEP 2—

STEP 3—

STEP 4—

This figure is walking toward you so that some of the shapes overlap each other. Get these steps down correctly before completing step 4.

PRINCESS FLORA

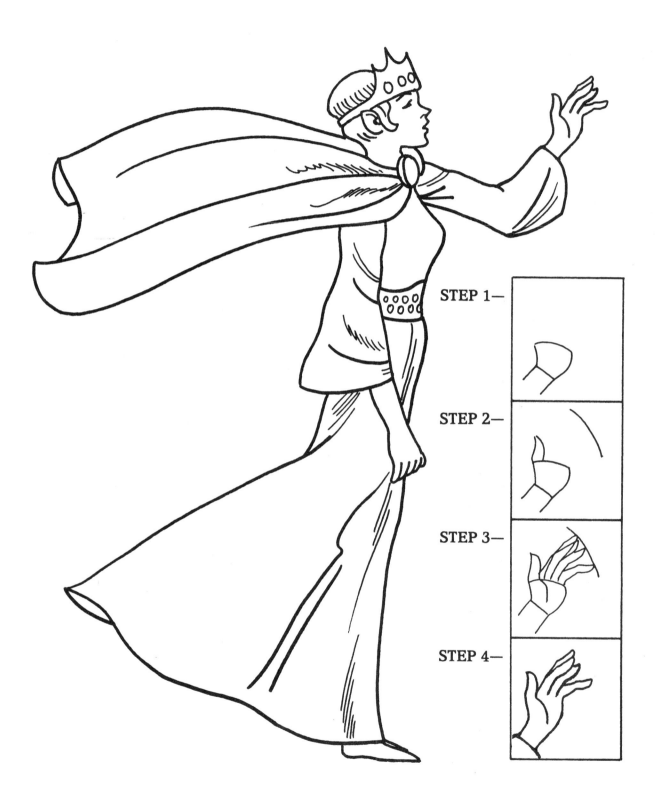

STEP 1—

STEP 2—

STEP 3—

STEP 4—

Hands are always difficult to draw, but just follow these steps and you'll draw this hand in no time at all.

STEP 1—

STEP 2—

STEP 3—

STEP 4—

The princess is 8 head shapes high. You must always draw the figure steps first before you add garments to it.

THE FLAMING ARROW

The light source for this figure is
the flaming arrow. Add your shadows
from these flames.

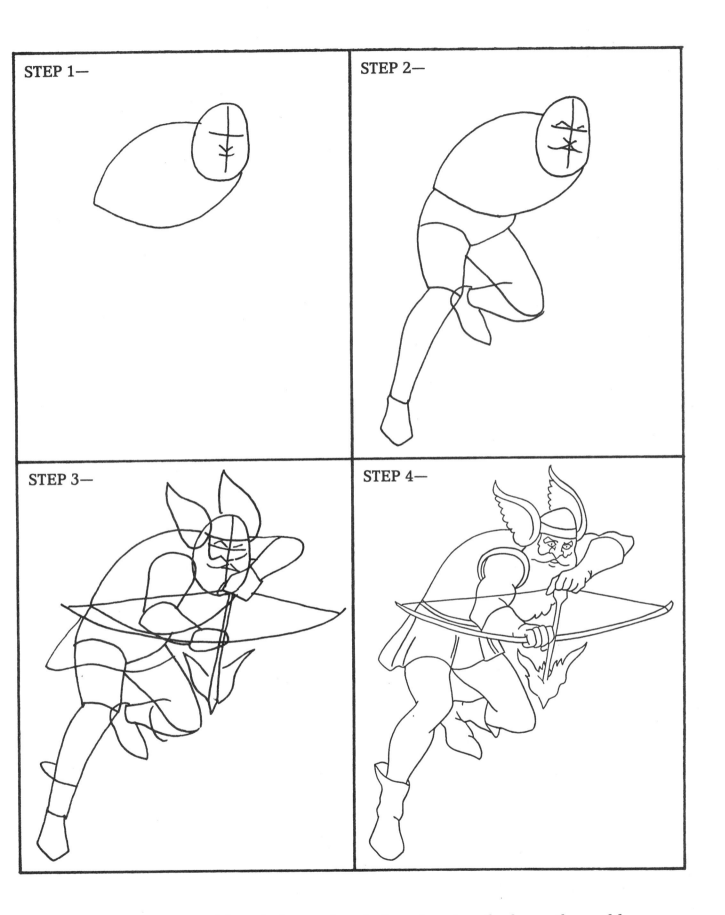

STEP 1—

STEP 2—

STEP 3—

STEP 4—

Draw the arm and hand shapes first before drawing the bow—then add
the arrow—then add the flames.

CLIMBING
SKULL CASTLE

Rendering the skull area with line and only
a few solid blacks, and then concentrating
the shadows on the figure only, gives the
picture a nice contrast.

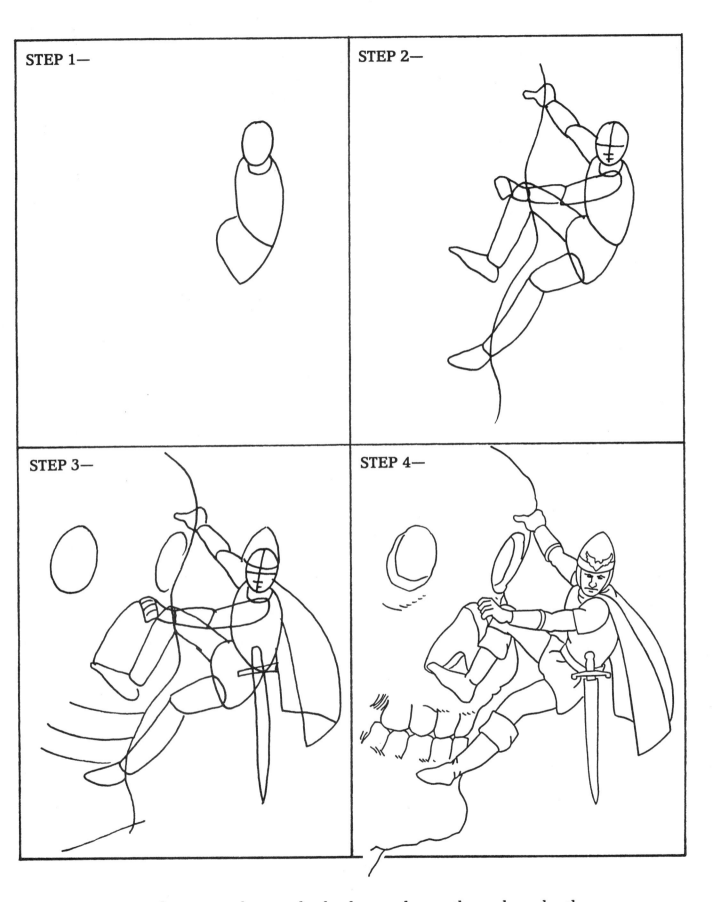

STEP 1—

STEP 2—

STEP 3—

STEP 4—

Notice that not only were body shapes drawn through each other, so was the background.

MASTER
MAGICIAN
MERLIN

Use the
light source
as a design
element in
this picture.

42

STEP 1—

STEP 2—

STEP 3—

STEP 4—

Get the drawing of the figure shapes done correctly before adding the mysterious form.

MERLIN, MASTER MAGICIAN

Decorate Merlin's costume with stars and moon crests and circle shapes.

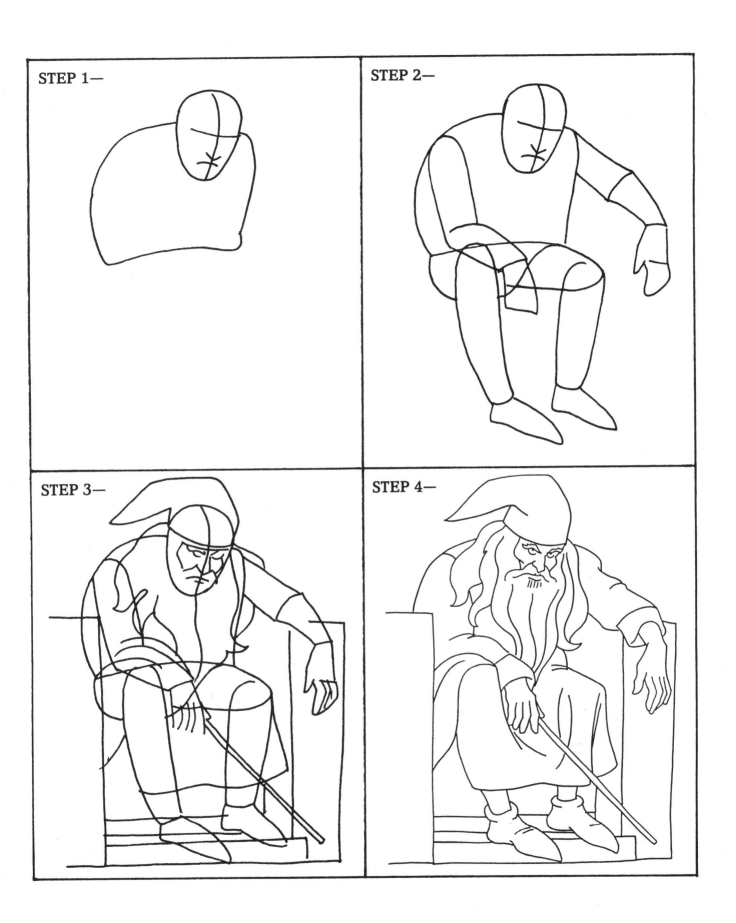

STEP 1—

STEP 2—

STEP 3—

STEP 4—

Draw Merlin's throne after you've drawn the figure shapes.

EVIL GOBLIN

Use the texture on his hat and suit to indicate they are made of fur.

STEP 1—

STEP 2—

STEP 3—

STEP 4—

This figure measures only 3½ head shapes high—just the right height for a goblin.

NESTOR

Make his face a
happy one. Render
the wood that he's
collected in line.

STEP 1—

STEP 2—

STEP 3—

STEP 4—

Nestor measures 3¼ head shapes high but he looks taller with his hat on.

THE CASTLE WITCH

This tone is made of a series of short lines.

Black areas and line tones have been used in a decorative manner.

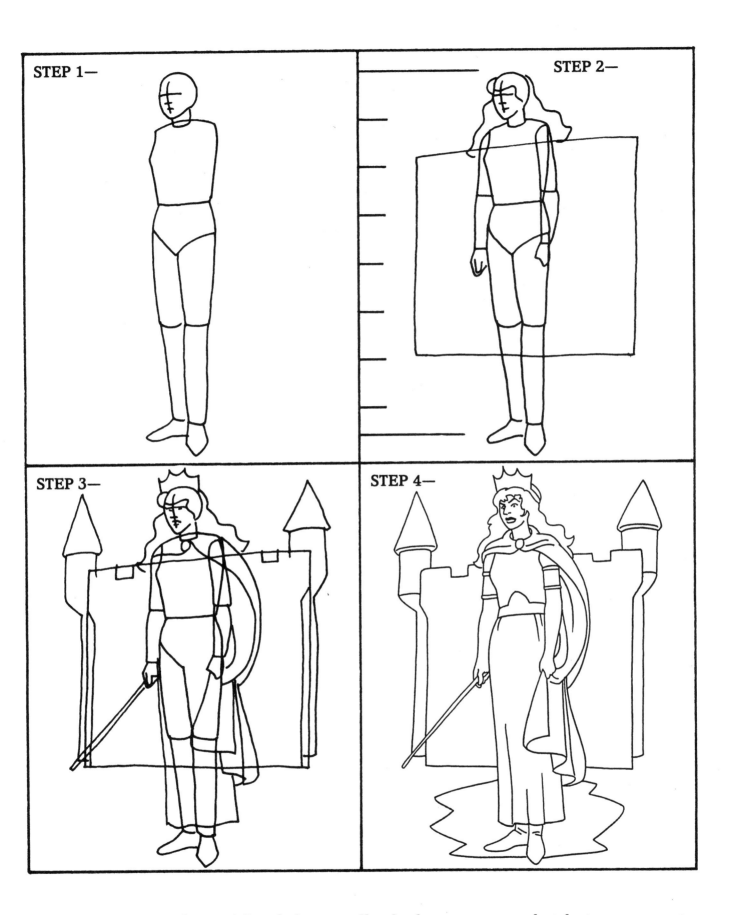

STEP 1—

STEP 2—

STEP 3—

STEP 4—

The witch is 7½ head shapes tall, which is an average height in drawing figures.

A TROLL
THIEF

A troll thief works in
the night, so here is
a time to use a lot of
dark shadows.

STEP 1—

STEP 2—

STEP 3—

STEP 4—

Add the hair and things that he has stolen only after the figure shapes have been properly drawn.

A TOWER GUARD

This is an example
of a very simple use
of black areas.

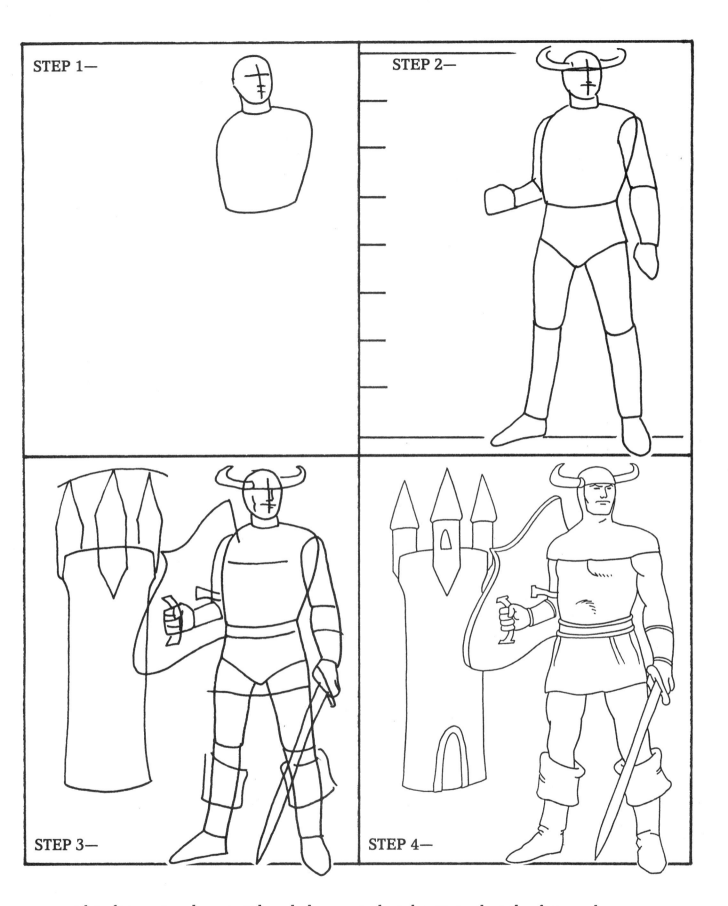

STEP 1—

STEP 2—

STEP 3—

STEP 4—

This figure is a heroic 8 head shapes in height. Note that the figure shapes have been drawn before the shield, sword and castle.

SKULL CASTLE

STEP 1—

STEP 2—

STEP 3—

STEP 4—

 Parallel vertical lines give the effect of water around the castle.
Blacks have only been used in great masses.
A series of various directional line strokes adds shadow.

KING DRYAD AND JASON

Keep the shadows simple in this complicated drawing.

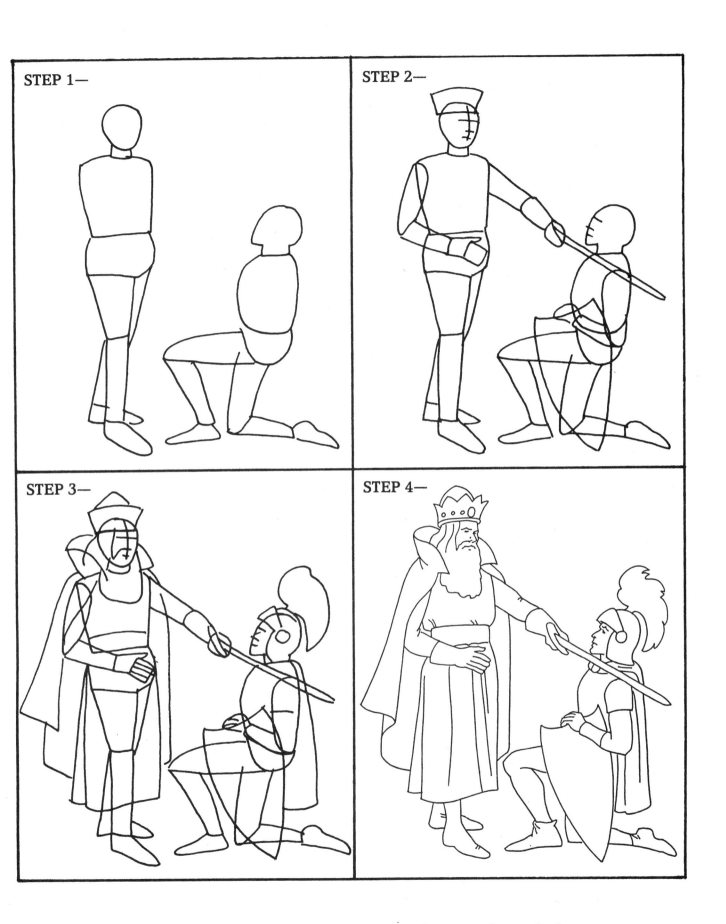

STEP 1—

STEP 2—

STEP 3—

STEP 4—

Draw each step as shown. Do not complete one figure before
beginning the other.

VICTORY

Draw action lines.

Keep the black areas on the figure only for contrast.

60

STEP 1—

STEP 2—

STEP 3—

STEP 4—

Draw the basic shapes of the figure before drawing the basic shapes of the dragon.

A BEAST FROM THE DUNGEON

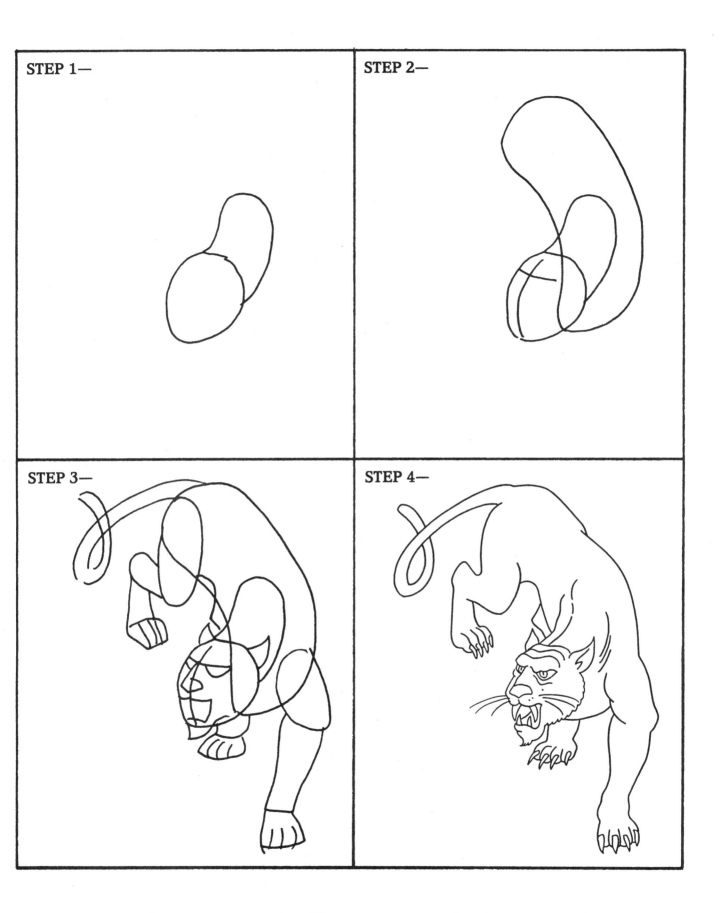

STEP 1—

STEP 2—

STEP 3—

STEP 4—

You use the same approach in drawing an animal or beast as you do in drawing a figure. Take one step at a time and don't be afraid to erase.

EMPIRE TRAVELER

The drawings on the next few pages are
somewhat more difficult. Concentrate on
the drawing and keep the shadows
and blacks simple.

STEP 1—

STEP 2—

STEP 3—

STEP 4—

Draw the basic shape of the creature first, then add the shapes
of the figure.

THE QUEEN'S WARRIOR

Add a cloud of
dust for action.

STEP 1—

STEP 2—

STEP 3—

STEP 4—

Draw the basic shape of the unicorn first, then add the shapes
of the figure.

WINGED WARRIOR

Add a few clouds to your
drawing for atmosphere.

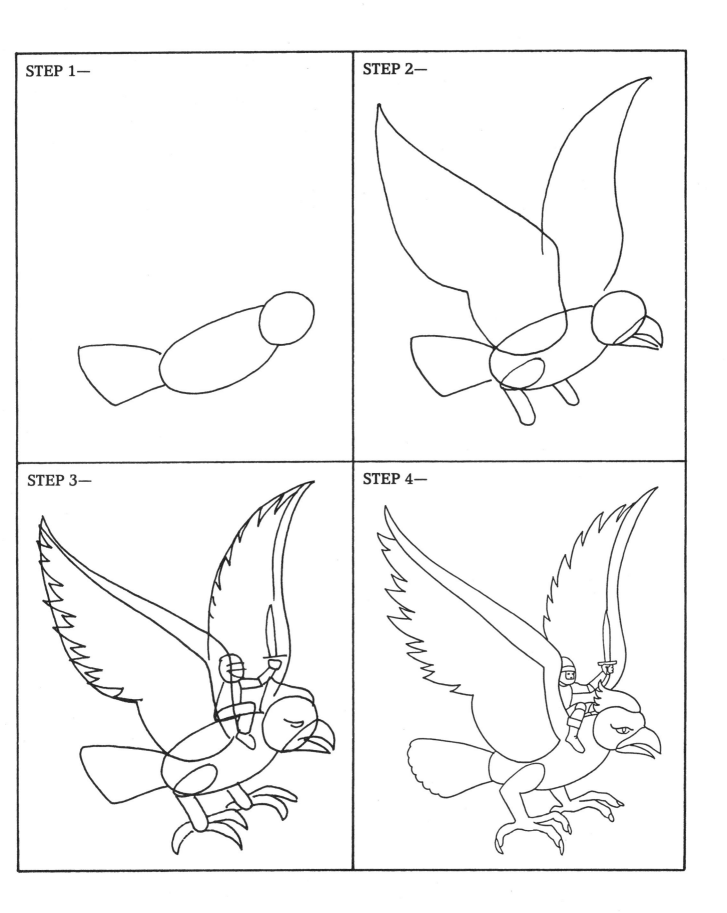

Draw the shapes of the body and wings first before drawing the shapes of the figure.

HOODED KNIGHT

Add action line
and a ground line.

STEP 1—

STEP 2—

STEP 3—

STEP 4—

Draw the shapes of the unicorn's body first, then draw the shapes of the
figure sitting on it. Don't be afraid to erase.

THE KING'S SENTRY

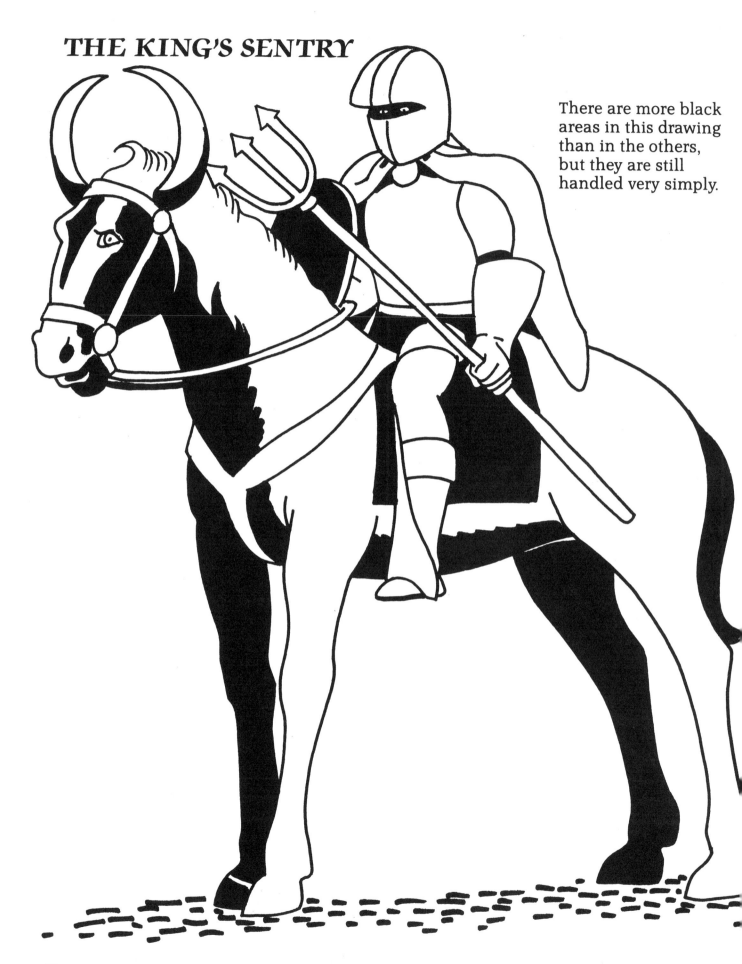

There are more black areas in this drawing than in the others, but they are still handled very simply.

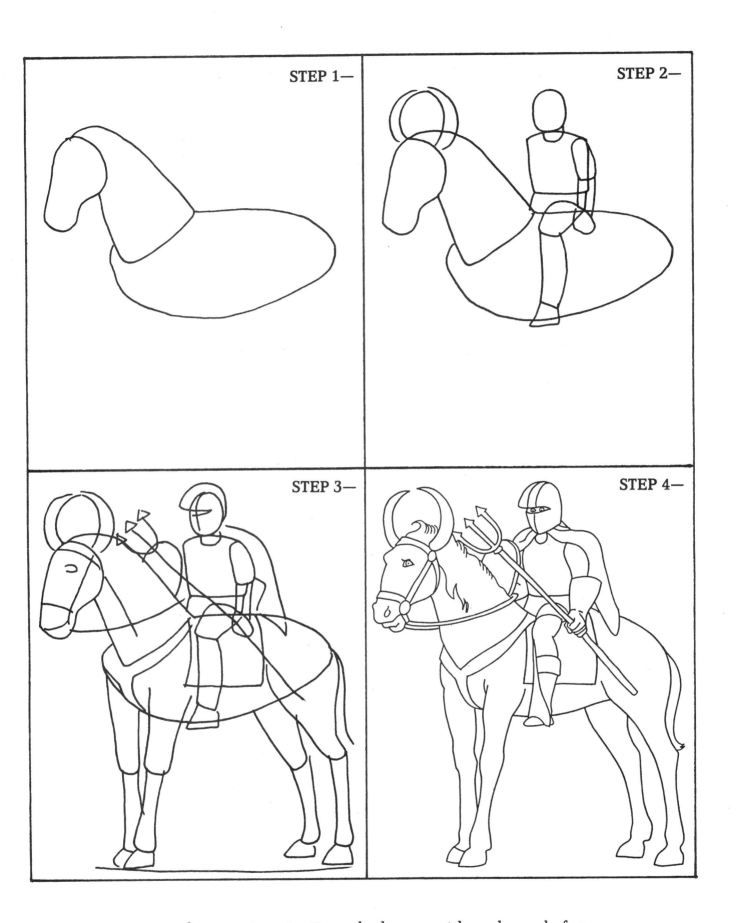

STEP 1—

STEP 2—

STEP 3—

STEP 4—

Just take one step at a time—be happy with each one before
you continue.

A BATTLE IN THE SKY

Draw these two on the same page for an action battle scene.

Keep the shadows simple.

STEP 1—

STEP 2—

STEP 3—

STEP 4—

STEP 1—

STEP 2—

STEP 3—

STEP 4—

75

THE BATTLE FOR THE EMPIRE

Establish a ground line for these gladiators.

Just take your time in doing this interactive drawing. Take one step at a time.

BATTLE OF THE KNIGHTS

STEP 1—

STEP 2—

STEP 3—

STEP 4—

Another interactive
battle in progress.

STEP 2—

STEP 1—

STEP 3—

STEP 4—

79

MILO IS READY FOR BATTLE

STEP 1—

Milo measures only about 4 head
shapes high.
The giant measures about 7½ head
shapes high.

STEP 2—

STEP 3—

STEP 4—

STEP 2—

STEP 1—

STEP 3—

STEP 4—

81

Now that you've learned to draw all these characters from Myths, Magic and Legends, here is a place for you to draw them to complete this story titled . . .

Merlin's Mission

JASON AND MILO WERE WALKING ALONG A DESERTED ROAD WHEN THE GREAT MAGICIAN MERLIN APPEARED IN THE SKY ABOVE THEM...

YOU MUST TRAVEL TO THE FORGOTTEN VALLEY AND RESCUE KING DRYAD'S DAUGHTER, PRINCESS FLORA! SHE IS BEING HELD BY THE EVIL EMPEROR ELECTRA AT SKULL CASTLE.

LOOK, JASON!

YOU CAN MAKE COPIES OF THESE PAGES SO AS NOT TO DRAW IN THIS BOOK.

DRAW MERLIN FROM PAGE 4 HERE.

"I'M NOT SURE ABOUT THIS," SAID MILO. "MERLIN CHOSE US OUT OF EVERYONE IN THE LAND TO RESCUE PRINCESS FLORA!" ANSWERED JASON.

YOU'RE RIGHT, JASON! WE MUSN'T LET HIM DOWN!

DRAW JASON AND MILO ON A UNICORN FROM PAGE 75 HERE.

NO SOONER HAD THEY ENTERED THE FORGOTTEN VALLEY WHEN THEY WERE GREETED BY A SOLDIER NAMED ZEUS. "MY GOOD FRIEND MERLIN TOLD ME YOU'D BE COMING THIS WAY," ZEUS SAID.

I CAN LEAD YOU TO SKULL CASTLE.

THANK YOU ZEUS!

DRAW ZEUS HERE FROM PAGE 24

THE THREE TRAVELED FOR SOME TIME BEFORE JASON REALIZED THAT SOMETHING WAS GOING TO GO WRONG. SUDDENLY, ZEUS BURST INTO FLAMES AND FILLED THE SKY WITH A MENACING SIGHT!

GO BACK!

IT'S A TRICK!

THAT'S NO FRIEND OF MERLIN!

DRAW THE EVIL MONSTER HERE FROM PAGE 6

BEFORE JASON AND MILO COULD REACT, THE CREATURE DISAPPEARED!
"UH-OH! SORRY I'M LATE, JASON. I COULD HAVE WARNED YOU ABOUT ZEUS,"
SAID A LITTLE VOICE FROM BEHIND A TREE.

WHO ARE YOU?

DON'T BE FRIGHTENED! I'M NESTOR, MERLIN'S HELPER.

DRAW NESTOR HERE FROM PAGE 48

"WHAT ARE YOU DOING HERE?" ASKED MILO. "I ALMOST FORGOT! I'VE BROUGHT
YOU A MAGIC SWORD DIRECTLY FROM MERLIN HIMSELF!" NESTOR REPLIED.

DRAW NESTOR WITH THE MAGIC SWORD HERE FROM PAGE 14

JASON CAREFULLY CLIMBED UP THE WALLS OF SKULL CASTLE TO REACH
THE ROOM WHERE PRINCESS FLORA WAS BEING HELD PRISONER.

DRAW JASON CLIMBING SKULL CASTLE HERE FROM PAGE 40

MEANWHILE MILO HELD OFF ONCOMING INTRUDERS.

DRAW MILO AND THE VICIOUS WARRIOR HERE FROM PAGES 80-81

JASON FREES THE PRINCESS.

COME WITH ME, PRINCESS FLORA. MY NAME IS JASON... I'M HERE TO RESCUE YOU!

DRAW PRINCESS FLORA HERE FROM PAGE 36

THROUGH DETERMINATION AND BRAVERY (NOT TO MENTION MERLIN'S MAGIC SWORD) JASON AND MILO WERE ABLE TO SAFELY BRING PRINCESS FLORA BACK TO HER FATHER, KING DRYAD.

I KING DRYAD KNIGHT YOU "JASON THE WARRIOR... BRAVEST PERSON IN ALL THE LAND!"

DRAW KING DRYAD AND JASON HERE FROM PAGE 58

We've only drawn
realistic figures,
dragons, trolls, etc.
up until now . . .

MYTHICAL MIRTH CARTOONS

STEP 1—

STEP 2—

STEP 3—

STEP 4—

Q: What do you feed a 25,000 pound dragon?
A: Everything it wants!

STEP 1—

STEP 2—

STEP 3—

STEP 4—

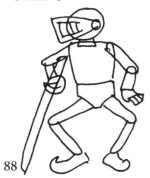

Q: How do knights in armor
approach dragons?
A: Very carefully!

Q: What etiquette problem do all dragons have?
A: Dragon breath!

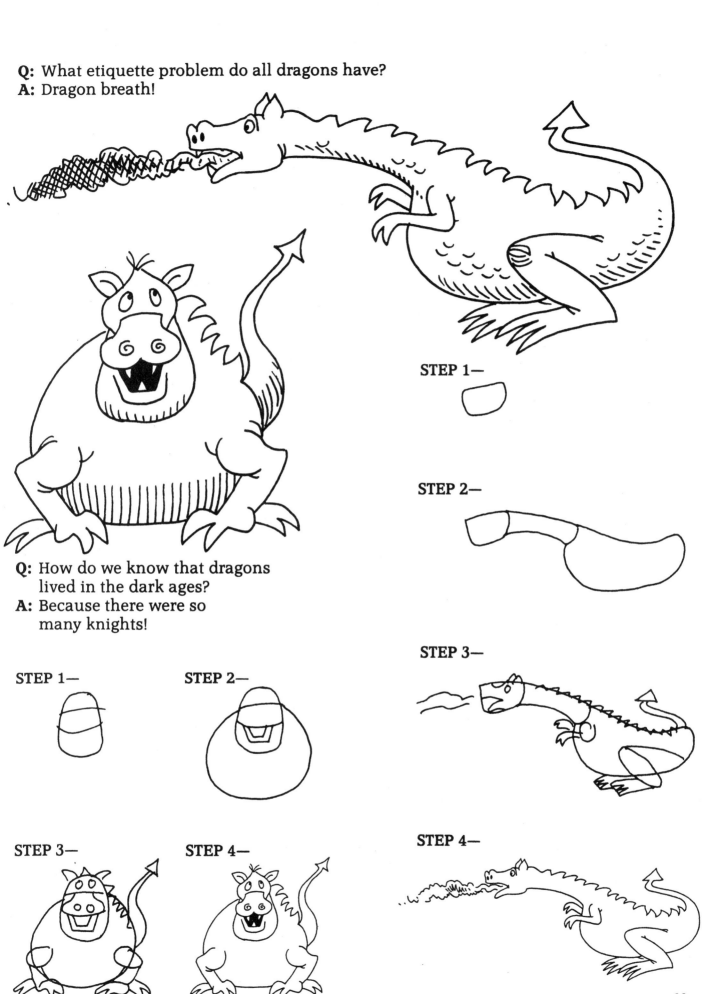

Q: How do we know that dragons
   lived in the dark ages?
A: Because there were so
   many knights!

STEP 1—

STEP 2—

STEP 3—

STEP 4—

STEP 1—

STEP 2—

STEP 3—

STEP 4—

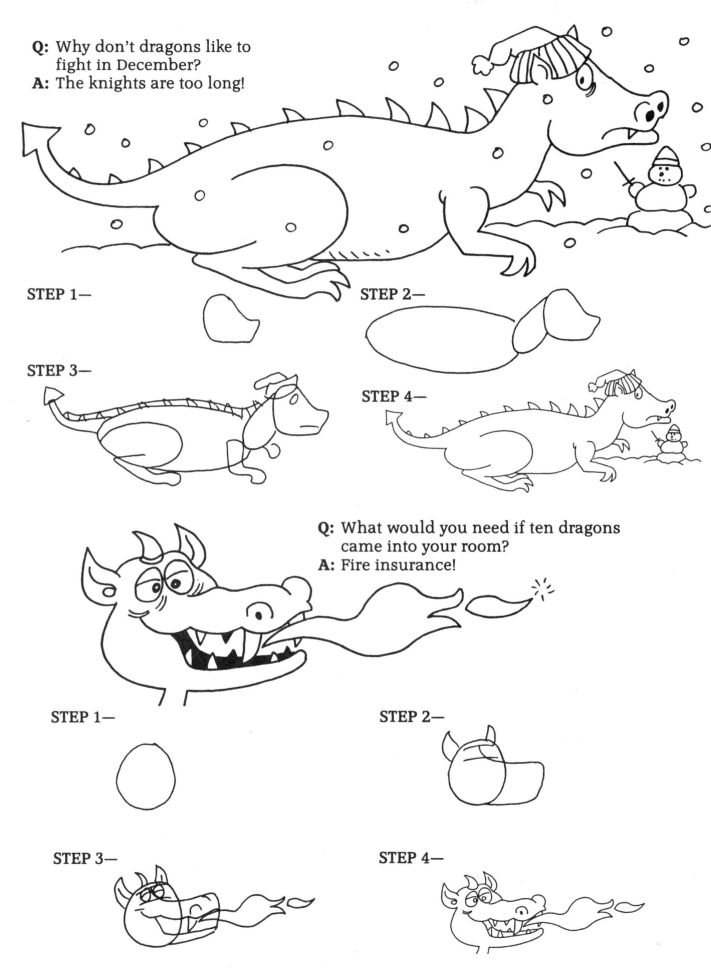

Q: Why don't dragons like to fight in December?
A: The knights are too long!

STEP 1—

STEP 2—

STEP 3—

STEP 4—

Q: What would you need if ten dragons came into your room?
A: Fire insurance!

STEP 1—

STEP 2—

STEP 3—

STEP 4—

Q: Do dragons have a sense of humor?
A: Yes! They try to make light of everything!

STEP 1—

STEP 2—

STEP 3—

STEP 4—

Q: Which sports do dragons like best?
A: All-knight games.

STEP 1—

STEP 2—

STEP 3—

STEP 4—

91

Q: Who makes the best dragon vampire victims?
A: People who like to stick out their necks.

STEP 1—

STEP 2—

STEP 3—

STEP 4—

Q: What do knights in armor suffer from?
A: Metal fatigue!

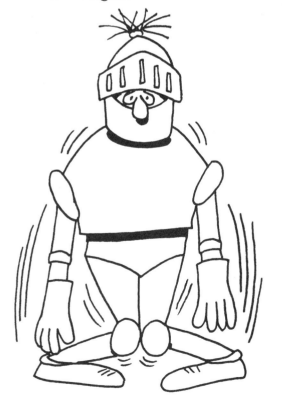

STEP 1—

STEP 2—

STEP 3—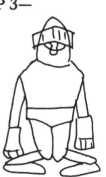

STEP 4—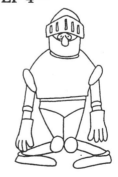